A WHISKER OF A TALE

BY

Jennifer René Daniel

Copyright 2013. All rights reserved.
P O Box 50207, Waterfront. 8002. South Africa.
jereleddaniel@gmail.com
ISBN: 978-1-920663-66-7

This book is dedicated to
my father
and mother,
Who made this world
a more beautiful place!

Whatsoever things are 'Pure!'
Think on 'these things!'

Phillipians 4:8

A WHISKER OF A TALE

BY

Jennifer René Daniel

CONTENTS

◆

	PAGE
Lady Jane	1
Molly	4
Squeaky	5
Tiddlywinks	6
Milly	7
Sally	8
Tippie Toes	9
Lady Jane	10
Noelie	11
Pretty Sue	12
Miss Knowall	13
Scurry	14
Sheila	15
Annie	16
Jenpen	17
Tiddle Toddle Toots	18
Essie & Francie	19
Roysticks	20
Brown Eyes	21
Aunt Abradagra	22
Lily Longsticks	23
Doodle Doring Doodlewood	24
Miss Jumper	25
Hilda	26

	PAGE
Beryl	27
Priscilla	28
Scurry	29
Sofia	30
Mary	31
Granny	32
Betty Blinkton Buttertoes	33
Jenny	34
Jenpen	35
Twinkletoes	36
Jerelé	37
Mary Jane	38
Joy	39
Esmerelda	40
Speedy Light'ning Rod	41
Sam	42
Royboy	43
Grandpa Gollick	44
Lady Agy	45
Green Goggle Annie	46
Tommy Traddle Toes	47
Trilly Trinket	48
Dorothy Dorkins	49
Tippie Tinderee	50
Amy	51
Ameliare Dunn	52
Esmerelda Hockingfoot	53
Frederick Wise	54
Pamela Primrose	55
Gertie Googly Gollidot	56
Lady Jane	57
Timothy Trundle	58
Mammy & Squeaky	59

	PAGE
Esmerelda	60
Kick Along Kickery	61
Little Lady Lilliput	62
Lady Jane	63
Dip Along Dippettie	64
Flippy	65
Flippy	66
Mr Comfitoes	67
Pinkie	68
Miss Quirkytell	69
Sally	70
Little Tilly Tender Mouse	71
Noelie	72
Ameliare Wintersocks	73

JENNIFER

RENÉ

DANIEL

Lady Jane

Lady Jane is sensitive of all her roles of fat!
Thus she wears a great big coat It covers up all that!

A WHISKER OF A TALE

Lady Jane

Lady Jane is fond of pink. She thinks it's feminine!
With it she is certain that; she'll approval win

Lady Jane

*Lady Jane has grown quite slim. She steps out in style
Dashing with her bright blue bow; nervous all the while!*

Molly

Molly is a shy young mouse who is scared that you
Won't allow her in your group. What is she to do?

A WHISKER OF A TALE

Squeaky

Squeaky is a homely mouse - always hard at work
Never will young squeaky mouse - any duty shirk!

A WHISKER OF A TALE

Tiddly-Winks

*Tiddlywinks is fond of green - for a party frock
With a little touch of pink - favourite of her stock!*

Milly

*Milly is a sweet young mouse - who will try her best
Though she hardly says a word - she outstrips the rest!*

A WHISKER OF A TALE

Sally

Sally is a brainy mouse - her eyes are hungry orbs!
Knowledge she observantly - constantly absorbs!

A WHISKER OF A TALE

Tippy Toes

*Always in a hurry - little Tippy Toes
Why she's always hurrying - no one really knows!*

A WHISKER OF A TALE

Lady Jane

Every inch a lady - from her head to toe
Therefore such a privilege - Lady Jane to know!

Noelie

They say the weather's very hot - but I am very cold!
I feel outdated in this suit - in fact it's very old!

Pretty Sue

*Quaint and precise in her garments of blue
Ever so capable sweet, pretty Sue!*

Miss Know All

*Listen dear children - to all that I say
I am Miss Know All - who bids you Good Day!*

A WHISKER OF A TALE

Scurry

Where are you running to, shy little mouse?
Have I upset you. Are you in a 'grouse?'

A WHISKER OF A TALE

Sheila

I am feeling ostracised. Wish I was not born!
Standing on the outskirts - loneliness, the norm!

Annie

I am going to a party, where there's lots of tea and cake
I sewed my pretty party dress. It was such fun to make!

Jenpen

*Guess what I'm thinking? I'm sure you can't tell
Thoughts that are sky high and deep as a well!*

Little Tiddle Toddle Toots is hoping you will be
Asking her to visit for a British cup of tea!

A WHISKER OF A TALE

Essie & Francie

Ever so different and yet much the same!
Two little sisters down memory lane

Roysticks

*Please don't forget me though you're far away!
Is it 'good-bye' or 'I'll see you some day?'*

Brown Eyes

Life is very dismal when your friends put you aside!
Why don't you and I set out - upon a great joy ride?

A WHISKER OF A TALE

Aunt Abradagra

*Aunt Abradagra has just had the flu
Buttoned and wrapped up - she still visits you!*

Lily Longsticks

*Dear Lily Longsticks is up in the clouds
She's going shopping to mix with the crowds!*

A WHISKER OF A TALE

Doodle Doring Doodlewood

Doodle Doring Doodlewood is passing down your street
'Absent-minded' he may pass - and not think to greet!

A WHISKER OF A TALE

Miss Jumper

*Children - It's time that we exercise limbs
Work off the fat and be turned into 'thins'!*

Hilda

I am rather sorry to be lording it o'er you!
But if one is uppercrust - that's what people do!

Beryl

I am the mouse with a listening ear!
Laughing when you laugh - and sharing each tear!

Priscilla

Let's get aquainted - I'd love to converse
On countless topics - before we disperse!

Scurry

*Is there a thing that you'd like me to do?
I would be happy to team up with you!*

A WHISKER OF A TALE

Sofia

Look, I am peeping to see if you guessed
That I'm unhappy and feeling depressed!

A WHISKER OF A TALE

Mary

*This highland lassie went out for a walk
The miles she sped o'er - has made people talk!*

Granny

Granny, you should visit - with your handbag full of sweets!
Peppermints and lemon drops and other fancy treats

Betty Blinkton Buttertoes

Betty Blinkton Buttertoes - has earned a sweet repose
She has been so busy - taking care of sickly Rose!

Jenny

I am quite desperate - for real English tea!
Give me a lift up and share some with me!

Jenpen

Please hurry up - I am last in the queue!
When one is desperate - what can one do?

A WHISKER OF A TALE

Twinkle Toes

I am just a little mouse - in mammy's 'grownup' clothes!
I feel very tiny - please don't laugh at Twinkle Toes!

Jerelé

I like to be quite out of view - beneath a large pink hat!
I am rather sensitive - but longing for a chat!

A WHISKER OF A TALE

Mary Jane

*Life seems quite pleasant to dear Mary Jane
Skipping and hopping through sunshine and rain!*

Joy

Joy is going to the shops - to buy a small green hat
Her jacket and her shoes are green - her bag too, fancy that!

Esmerelda

It is so hard - to leave youth far behind!
Why not to age - be a little bit blind!

Speedy Light'ning Rod

*Master Speedy Light'ning Rod - my name you surely know
Quick and sharp in all I do - in sport a famous pro!*

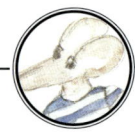

A WHISKER OF A TALE

Sam

The tricks I've tried have highs and lows
The price to pay - each sportsman knows!

Royboy

Life has many turnings - as we all so surely know!
'Milestones' point us further - on the road we have to go!

Grandpa Gollick

Old Grandpa Gollick is riddled with pain!
Gout that has come on - because of the rain!

A WHISKER OF A TALE

Lady Agy

Dear Lady Agy has been rather bored!
I've kept her waiting - will peace be restored?

A WHISKER OF A TALE

Green Goggle Annie

Green Goggle Annie says it's quite absurd
To slay the English tongue! Use the right word

Tommy Traddle Toes

*Little Tommy Traddle Toes gives his side a rub
To alleviate the pain - caused by a golf club!*

A WHISKER OF A TALE

Trilly Trinket

See how the housework has injured my spine!
Says Trilly Trinket - forgive if I whine!

Dorothy Dorkins

Dorothy Dorkins is such a sweet mouse
Truly 'the princess' who lives in our house!

A WHISKER OF A TALE

Tippee Tinderee

Trendy Tippee Tinderee has come as a new guest
Pretty as a picture - she is shy of all the rest!

A WHISKER OF A TALE

Amy

Amy is a solemn mouse who's always thinking deeply
When she speaks we listen - as 'home truths' are given sweetly!

A WHISKER OF A TALE

Ameliare Dunn

My little darling Ameliare Dunn
Where, tell me where, have your little feet run?

Esmerelda Hockingfoot

Esmerelda Hockingfoot is walking down the street
With her nose up in the air - no-one will she greet!

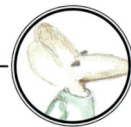

A WHISKER OF A TALE

Frederick Wise

Life is such fun - to young Frederick Wise
Energy bursting in each enterprise!

A WHISKER OF A TALE

Pamela Primrose

Pamela Primrose is waiting for you
To bid her welcome - the friendship renew!

Gertie Googly Gollidot

Gertie Gertie Gollidot - is fond of playing ball.
If you'd like to join her - you must quickly make a call.

Lady Jane

*Lady Jane has mastered such a stylish mode of dress
That she has succeeded - in her longing to impress!*

A WHISKER OF A TALE

Timothy Trundle

Timothy Trundle is bored with his rest
So much he almost - would welcome a test!

A WHISKER OF A TALE

*Come my little darling - throw that heavy tennis ball
I will try to hit it. On the ground it may not fall!*

A WHISKER OF A TALE

Esmerelda

Will you come and join me in this game of tennisette?
But you must be patient - if the ball lands in the net!

Kick Along Kickery

*Kick Along Kickery's the smartest mouse
When he performs - he will bring down the house!*

A WHISKER OF A TALE

Little Lady Lilliput

Little Lady Lillyput is wondering if she
Should go walking down the road - or stay and talk with me!

Lady Jane

Lady Jane's sad as she comes home from town
Nowhere, could she find a fluffy pink gown!

A WHISKER OF A TALE

Dip Along Dippettie

Dip Along Dippettie's rigged out in blue!
Is it because she has just had the flu?

Flippy

*Life is like a tightrope - that we have to walk
Flippy is so grateful - for her wooden stalk!*

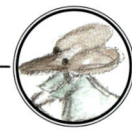

A WHISKER OF A TALE

Flippy

Flippy just laughs - as she triples along
Life is for her - a continual song!

A WHISKER OF A TALE

Mr Comfitoes

*Do not dare to mess around - with Mr Comfitoes!
He has studied copiously - and knows how much he knows!*

Pinkie

In my little pocket of a soft pink shade
Tiny little peppermints that I can raid!

Miss Quirkytell

Children do listen - to Miss Quirkytell
Reach up above - if you want to serve well!

A WHISKER OF A TALE

Sally

Come out - have fun - it's a glorious day!
That's why I'm skipping - the whole of the way!

Little Tilly Tender Mouse

*Little Tilly Tendermouse just loves a cup of tea
Often she has quickly made - a pot for her and me!*

A WHISKER OF A TALE

Noelie

I feel so lonely and caged in today!
Why don't you join me - inside here to play?

Ameliare Wintersocks

Come and help this lonely mouse - Ameliare Wintersocks
If you do not rescue her - she'll land upon the rocks!

A WHISKER OF A TALE

The End

A WHISKER OF A TALE